First Questions and Answers about the **Beach**

# How Big Is the Ocean?

TIME
LIFE *for*
*Children*®

ALEXANDRIA, VIRGINIA

# Contents

# Why is the beach sandy?

A sandy beach feels soft, but a long time ago it was made of hard rocks. Waves slowly pulled the rocks into the water. Then the rocks tumbled against each other, breaking into smaller pieces. Finally the pieces became tiny grains of sand, and waves washed the sand up onto the beach.

**Did you know?**

Some beaches are white or pink because they are made of broken shells or coral, not broken rocks. Other beaches may be green or red or black.

# Why is the water blue?

Water has no color at all, but on a bright day the sun makes it look blue. Sunlight is made of many colors, including blue. When sunlight hits the water, most of these colors are absorbed, or swallowed up. Only the blue bounces off the water and reaches our eyes, so the water looks blue.

**Try it!**
When you're at the beach, scoop some water into a pail and look at it. Does it still look blue?

# Why is the ocean so cold?

Water takes a long time to heat up—much longer than air. When summer comes, the air above the beach gets hot, but the water in the ocean is still cool. Because your body is hot from standing on the beach, the water feels extra cold when you go in it.

*Cold water doesn't bother me! I have oil on my feathers that keeps me dry!*

9

# What makes waves?

Waves are made by the wind, which blows over the
ocean and wrinkles it. As the wind blows a wave
toward the sloping shore, the bottom of the wave
starts to go slower than the top. This makes
the wave topple over, and it hits the beach with a
CRASH! If the wave is small, it makes a sound
like a whisper.

**_Try it!_**

Put some water in a shallow pan.
Blow gently across the top.
Do you see waves?

# What makes ocean water salty?

The salt in the ocean comes from rocks on land. As a river flows over these rocks, it washes the salt out of them. The river carries the salt to the ocean, where it makes the seawater taste salty.

*That's the wrong kind of water — don't drink it!*

**Did you know?**

It's much easier to float in salt water than it is in fresh water.

# Where do clams live?

A clam digs itself into the sand with a strong muscle called a foot. Once it is deep enough to feel safe, the clam stretches a pair of long tubes up to the surface of the sand. Food and water pour into one of these tubes when the waves come in. The clam squirts water out through the other tube.

**Did you know?**
Tiny holes at the water's edge may mean
that clams are hiding below. The clams
make the holes when they squirt out water.

# How big is the ocean?

The ocean is bigger than anything else in the world. That's because most of the planet we live on is covered by water. The earth is really one big ocean with chunks of land sticking up out of the water.

# What are those people trying to catch?

Any fish that comes close enough! But that's not many. Most fish live farther out at sea, where they can find more to eat.

**Salmon** go back to rivers to lay their eggs. When the eggs hatch, the young salmon swim to the ocean.

**Flounders** are as flat as pancakes. Their shape lets them hide on the sandy bottom, waiting for food.

**Striped bass** have beautiful bars on their bodies.

Little fish like **herring** swim in big groups, called schools.

*A flounder changes color to hide. Can you find any flounders here?*

# Where do crabs live?

Crabs are lucky: They can live in two places! Like fish, they have gills that let them live and breathe underwater. But their bodies also use air, so they can crawl around on dry land. Crabs love tide pools–places where the ocean waves leave puddles of water on the beach. The waves bring in lots of plants and animals for the crabs to eat.

21

# Do other animals live at the beach?

Many wonderful creatures live on, under, or near the beach. Each one of them is specially suited for ocean life.

A **barnacle** may look dead, but inside its shell is a live animal.

**Starfish** use suction cups to hold onto rocks. **Mussels** stay attached by tough threads.

**Scallops** squirt water to move – especially when a starfish is chasing them!

**Terns** and **pelicans** soar above the waves and swoop down to grab fish.

**Sandpipers** like to dig for worms and mole crabs.

A **seasnail** pulls itself along with its foot.

**Clams** hide by digging into the sand.

23

# What are all those birds doing?

They're looking for something to eat! Each bird has just the right beak to get the food it's after.

**Pelicans** dive into the water and scoop fish into their big beaks. A pelican can hold more fish in its beak than it can in its stomach!

The **sanderling** digs up cockles and pries open the shells with its beak.

A **laughing gull** can sit on a pelican's head and steal fish right out of its mouth!

The **willet** uses its beak like a spear to stab fish.

**Plovers** use their beaks to peck beach fleas from the sand for their dinner.

25

# Why do seashells have different shapes?

Some sea creatures make their own shells. A liquid comes out of the animal's body and hardens around it, forming a shell that is shaped like the animal inside. A creature with a flat body makes a flat shell. A creature that curls its body as it grows makes a coiled shell. When the animal dies, its shell is left behind for you to find.

Razor clam

Moon snail

Scallop

Whelk

Jingle shell

Clam

Pen

Slipper

Angel wings

**Try it!**

If you find a conch shell like this on the beach, hold it up to your ear. You'll hear a noise inside it that sounds like ocean waves.

Periwinkle

Cockle

# What else can I find on the beach?

Many of the things that wash up on the beach tell about life at sea.

Pieces of **coral** come from a big group of corals, called a colony. Corals are animals, not plants!

*I wonder why humans think beachcombing is so much fun!*

A skate egg was inside this **mermaid's purse.**

**Feathers** from all kinds of birds can be found drying in the sun.

*Did you know?*
Never pick up garbage if you find any
on the beach; tell a grownup about it instead.

Tree trunks or branches that have been tossed
by waves become smooth **driftwood.**
Sunlight and salt water have turned the
driftwood white or gray.

Waves and sand rub the sharp edges
off broken pieces of glass and turn
them into frosted **beach glass**.

# Where does seaweed come from?

Seaweed is a plant that grows in the ocean. Some seaweeds, such as whip weed, look like ropes. Others, such as kelp, are rippled like lasagne noodles. And some, such as gulfweed, have air sacs that help them float. When seaweed gets washed into a tide pool on the beach, periwinkles and hermit crabs use it as a hiding place.

*That's not real lettuce— that's sea lettuce!*

Kelp

Whip weed

Gulf weed

31

# Do other plants grow near the beach?

All sorts of plants grow in the sand near a beach. Some of them are hard to see because they grow just above the ground. Growing close to the ground keeps them from getting pulled out of the sand by the wind. Other beach plants bend over when the wind blows, then stand back up when the wind dies down.

Scratchy **sandburs** can stick to towels, blankets, or you!

**Reeds** and **cattails** grow in salt marshes and salt ponds.

**Sea oats** grow on sand dunes.
They help to hold the sand in place.

Wild **roses** spill over the dunes.
Their seeds, called rose hips,
can be made into jelly.

35

# Why is the beach so windy?

The air above the beach is usually a different temperature from the air above the ocean. When cold air bumps into warm air, the air starts moving around. Another name for moving air is wind. This steady wind makes the beach a great place to fly a kite!

35

# What is a sand dune?

A dune is a big pile of sand that was pushed into place by the wind. Some sand dunes are covered with grass or flowers or sea oats. The roots of these plants keep the sand from blowing away.

# Why can't I play on the dunes?

Because climbing on the sand can make it slide away!
Sand dunes protect the land and houses behind the beach
from strong winds coming off the sea. Animals and
insects live in the dunes, too. If the sand dunes blew
away, all kinds of creatures would have no place to live!

**Did you know?**
A sand dune takes years and years to grow,
but a big storm can destroy it in a day!

# How come dry sand doesn't make good castles?

Dry sand doesn't hold together. The grains slip and slide against each other, just as they do on a dune. But when grains of sand are coated with water, they stick together. That's why a castle built with wet sand is strong enough to hold up a flag.

41

**Try it!**

To see how water makes dry things stick together, stir some dry flour in a bowl. What happens? Now add some water and stir again. What is the difference?

# Why does water come into the holes I dig?

Waves splash onto the beach all day and all night. Most of this water slides back into the sea, but some of it soaks into the sand. That's why there's always plenty of water right beneath the sand at the edge of the ocean. It's a good thing, too—sand creatures use that water to stay alive!

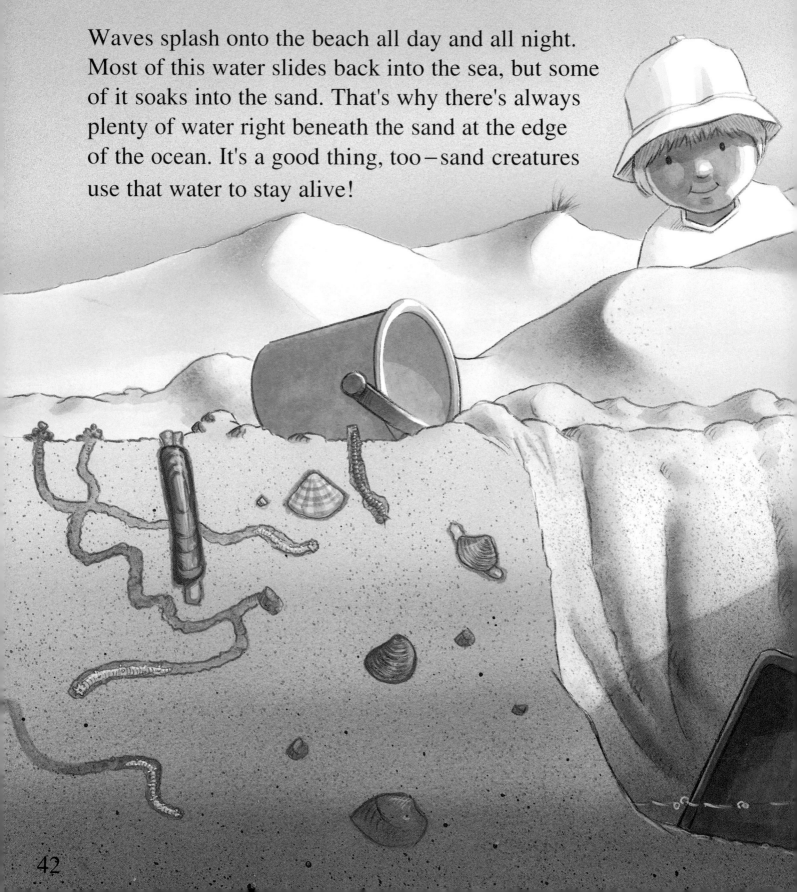

**Try it!**
When you visit the beach, dig a hole in the sand far back from the water. Feel the sand. Now dig another hole close to the water. How does it feel?

43

# Why is the water coming up the beach?

You may not notice it, but the ocean is always moving slowly toward the land or slowly away from it. These movements are called tides. When the water has moved up the beach as far as it can, it is high tide. When the water has moved down the beach as far as it can, it is low tide.

**Try it!**
Low tide is a good time to look for rocks and shells that the ocean has uncovered.

# What happens on the beach at night?

The people go home, but the animals stay busy. Ghost crabs run sideways, looking for food. Black skimmers fly along with their beaks in the water to catch fish. Sea turtles crawl out of the ocean to lay their eggs in the sand. The beach grass moves with the wind and sounds like it is whispering.

Sleep Tight!
Don't let the
Beach fleas bite!

**TIME-LIFE for CHILDREN**®

**Managing Editor:** Patricia Daniels
**Editorial Directors:** Jean Burke Crawford, Allan Fallow,
　　　　　　　　　　　Karin Kinney, Sara Mark
**Senior Art Director:** Susan K. White
**Editorial Coordinator:** Marike van der Veen
**Editorial Assistant:** Mary M. Saxton
**Production Manager:** Marlene Zack
**Senior Copyeditor:** Colette Stockum
**Production:** Celia Beattie

**Quality Assurance Manager:** Miriam P. Newton

**Library:** Louise D. Forstall, Anne Heising

**Special Contributor:** Barbara Klein
**Researcher:** Jocelyn Lindsay
**Writer:** Jacqueline A. Ball

**Designed by:** 　**David Bennett Books Ltd**
**Series design:** 　David Bennett
**Book design:** 　David Bennett
**Art direction:** 　David Bennett
**Illustrated by:** 　Michael Brownlow
**Additional cover**
　**illustrations by:** Nick Baxter

First printing. Printed in U.S.A.
Published simultaneously in Canada.

Time Life Inc. is a wholly owned subsidiary of THE TIME INC. BOOK COMPANY.

TIME-LIFE is a trademark of Time Warner Inc. U.S.A.

For subscription information, call 1-800-621-7026.

School and library distribution by Time-Life Education,
P.O. Box 85026, Richmond, VA 23285-5026.

**Library of Congress Cataloging-in-Publication Data**
How big is the Ocean? : first questions and answers about
the beach.
p. cm. (Time-Life library of first questions and answers)
ISBN 0-7835-0897-2 　(hardcover)
1. Beaches--Juvenile Literature. [1. Beaches.]
I. Time-Life for Children (Firm) II. Series: Library of first questions and answers.

GB453.H69 1994
508.3146--dc20 　　　　　　　　　　　　　　94-26840
　　　　　　　　　　　　　　　　　　　　　　　CIP
　　　　　　　　　　　　　　　　　　　　　　　AC

## Consultants

**Dr. Lewis P. Lipsitt**, an internationally recognized specialist in childhood development, was the 1990 recipient of the Nicholas Hobbs Award for science in the service of children. He has served as the science director for the American Psychological Association and is a professor of psychology and medical science at Brown University.

**Thomas D. Mullin** directs the Beaver Brook Association in Hollis, New Hampshire, where he coordinates workshops and seminars designed to promote appreciation for wildlife and the environment.

**Dr. Judith A. Schickedanz**, an authority on the education of preschool children, is an associate professor of early childhood education at the Boston University School of Education, where she also directs the Early Childhood Learning Laboratory. Her published work includes *More Than the ABCs: Early Stages of Reading and Writing Development* as well as several textbooks and many scholarly papers.